KEEPING SAFE

ONLINE

by Anne Rooney

W
FRANKLIN WATTS
LONDON • SYDNEY

First published in 2014 by Franklin Watts

Copyright © Arcturus Holdings Limited

Franklin Watts
338 Euston Road
London NW1 3BH
Franklin Watts Australia
Level 17/207 Kent Street, Sydney NSW 2000

Produced by Arcturus Publishing Limited,
26/27 Bickels Yard, 151–153 Bermondsey Street, London SE1 3HA

Editors: Penny Worms and Joe Harris
Designer: Emma Randall
Cover designer: Emma Randall
Original design concept: Elaine Wilkinson

Picture credits: All images courtesy of Shutterstock.

A CIP catalogue record for this book is available from the British Library.

Dewey Decimal Classification Number 004.6'78

ISBN 978 1 4451 3250 1
Printed in China

Franklin Watts is a division of Hachette Children's Books,
an Hachette UK company.

www.hachette.co.uk

SL004067UK
Supplier 03, Date 0614, Print Run 3440

CONTENTS

HAVING A HAPPY ONLINE LIFE

Going online can be great fun. You can use your computer, tablet or phone to socialize with friends, play games, watch videos and help with homework. However, when you are online, you need to be sensible and careful to keep yourself safe.

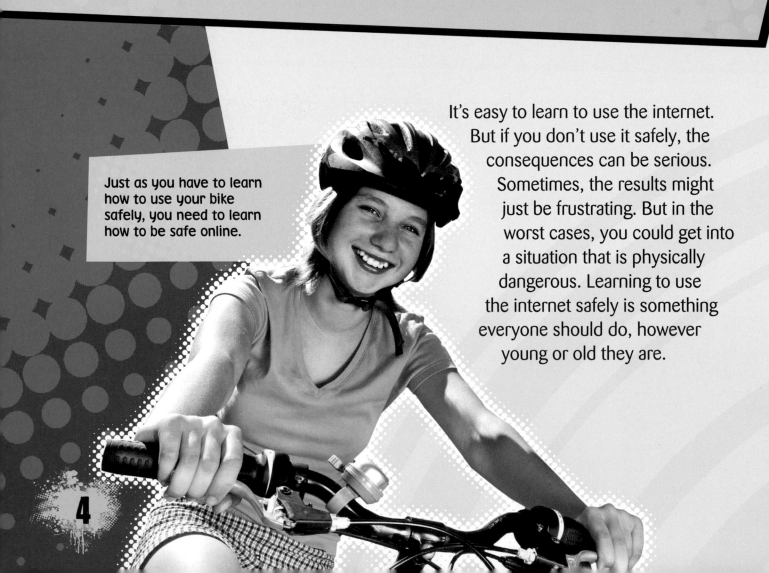

Just as you have to learn how to use your bike safely, you need to learn how to be safe online.

It's easy to learn to use the internet. But if you don't use it safely, the consequences can be serious. Sometimes, the results might just be frustrating. But in the worst cases, you could get into a situation that is physically dangerous. Learning to use the internet safely is something everyone should do, however young or old they are.

SAFETY TIP

It's easy to get carried along by things other people are doing. Make sure you don't get drawn into cruel online behaviour. Remember that what you say on the net will affect people in the real world.

Some dangers on the internet are directed at particular people. A **cyberbully** – someone who uses the internet to bully people – usually picks out a specific person to bully (their **target**). Other dangers are more general. For example, some emails encourage you to click on links that might damage your computer. They are usually sent out randomly to a large number of email addresses.

If you know how to behave safely online, you can have lots of fun with friends.

5

CYBERBULLYING

There are bullies online, just as there are bullies in the real world. Online bullying is called cyberbullying. It is repeated, unkind behaviour that is done on purpose to upset someone. Although it doesn't cause physical harm, it is very upsetting because it can happen at any time – even when you are at home.

Cyberbullying takes many forms. It can be nasty messages sent by phone or email. It can include being **abusive** or ridiculing someone on a social networking site, perhaps by posting embarrassing photos or videos of them. Lots of people might join in, making it even more upsetting. Leaving someone out of online activity such as chats or games is also cyberbullying.

Most phones let you block numbers you don't want to be contacted from, and that's a good way to stop upsetting messages or calls.

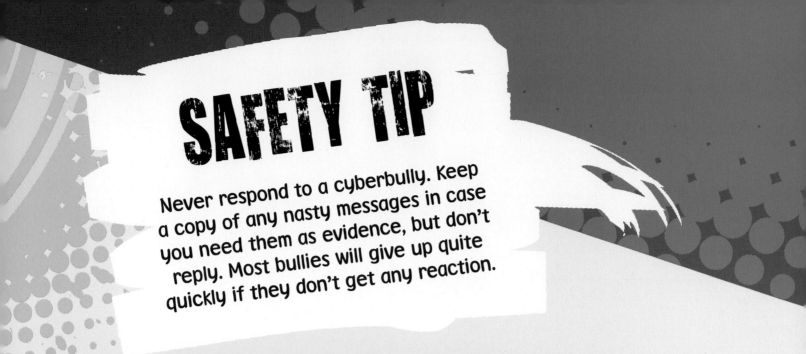

SAFETY TIP

Never respond to a cyberbully. Keep a copy of any nasty messages in case you need them as evidence, but don't reply. Most bullies will give up quite quickly if they don't get any reaction.

Sometimes, a cyberbully might **hijack** an **account** to send messages or post photos in someone else's name. At the very least, this can be annoying, but at worst it can cause a great deal of trouble and upset in the real world. Always log out of your account when you finish using a shared computer. Change your online passwords if anyone guesses them.

If someone bullies you online, always tell a grown-up and ask for help dealing with it.

USING SOCIAL MEDIA SAFELY

Social networking sites offer a great way of keeping in touch with friends and family, especially those who live far away. Some sites, such as Facebook and Twitter, have a minimum age for users. If you are below that age, it's better to use a site specifically for younger people. These are the ones that protect you the best.

Be careful who you accept as an online friend. It's best only to 'friend' people who you know and like in the real world. Remember that you don't really know someone if your only contact with them is online. People can pretend to be someone they are not and you have no way of knowing.

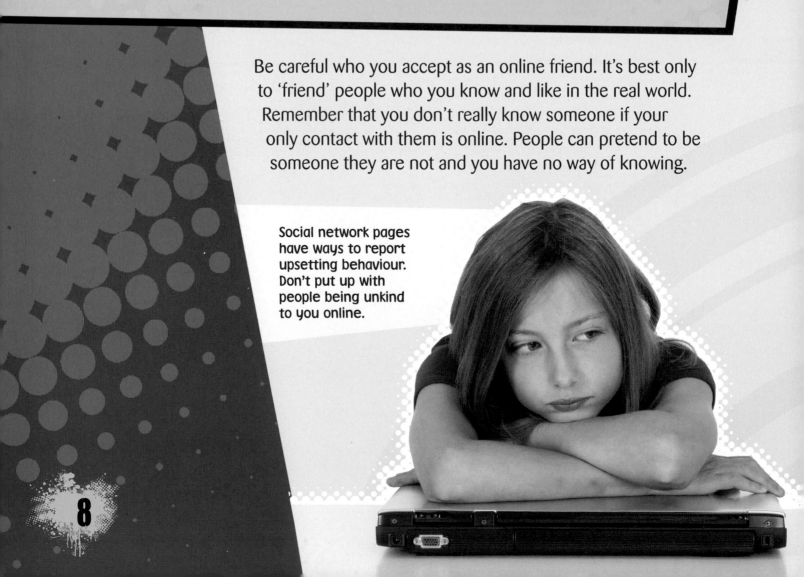

Social network pages have ways to report upsetting behaviour. Don't put up with people being unkind to you online.

SAFETY TIP

It's best not to use a photo of yourself as your main profile image on a chat or social networking site. A photo of your pet, your favourite band or a cartoon character keeps your identity private from strangers.

If people are mean to you or about you on social media sites, tell them you don't like it and ask them to stop. If they carry on, you can **de-friend** them and block them. You should also report nasty messages as abuse – there is usually a button or option to do this.

It's great to take your real-world friendships online so you can share photos, videos and information.

SHARE CAREFULLY

Socializing online is different from chatting with friends face to face, because what you say can often be seen by many other people. It can sometimes be difficult to tell whether a post or comment is visible only to friends, or whether it is going out to a wider audience. That audience might include complete strangers.

Be careful about what you share online. Never post your phone number, address or email address on a website, unless you are absolutely sure that it is private. You can use online **privacy settings** to keep your information visible only to your friends.

If you are 'tagged' in a photo or video, it's easy to remove the tag and no one can retag you.

SAFETY TIP

You can skip questions when you set up your profile page on a social networking site. It's safest to leave your address, email, school and phone number blank.

Any **personal information** that you post online could help a stranger identify you or find you in the real world. This means you have to be careful with photos, too. Don't share photos that show where you live or which school you go to. Details like that could help a stranger track you down.

If you think a friend might be embarrassed by a photograph you post, check with them before uploading it.

KEEP YOUR INFORMATION SAFE

If someone else gains access to your online accounts, they can use them as if they were you. They can **disrupt** your online life, for example by uploading offensive photos and posting things in your name. If someone posts upsetting images or abusive messages in your name, you may get in trouble.

If you use a public or shared computer – such as at school or in a library – remember to log out of your account when you've finished. If you don't, the next person will be able use your account. If this happens to you, you should tell a trusted adult what has happened, try to change your password, and contact the website's support team.

You need to be 16 to buy online. If you want a parent to buy you something, ask them to check carefully what you are buying and make sure it's a safe site.

SAFETY TIP

Set up your mobile phone so that no one can use it without a password. Otherwise, if you lose your phone or have it stolen, someone else will be able to use your online accounts.

A good way to keep your information and accounts safe is to choose strong passwords. Make sure you pick passwords that other people can't guess, and don't write them down where it's obvious they are passwords. Don't use the same password for everything – if someone finds or guesses it, they can take over all your accounts.

If other people watch you log in, they might see and remember your password.

ONLINE CHAT

Online chat is a great way to keep in touch with friends or family you don't see very often, but be careful who you chat to. It's not safe to chat to people you don't know in the real world. Online, people can easily pretend to be someone they're not. Even their photo could be of someone else.

Never give out personal information online, or tell anyone where you are. It's dangerous to meet someone you have befriended online, even if you truly believe the person is genuine. You may have become good online friends but always check with a parent before arranging a meeting. Never meet up with someone in secret and alone.

It's fine to use a webcam with your family and close friends, but don't use it with strangers.

SAFETY TIP

Don't chat to people you don't know, especially if they ask for a private chat. It doesn't matter if they seem nice or funny. They may be lying and not very nice at all.

You really don't know who someone is if you only know them online

Sometimes, an adult befriends a young person with the intention of doing them harm. They might pretend to be someone else to win the trust of a young person and then try to meet up with them to hurt them. This is called 'grooming'. It can happen online or in the real world.

STAY IN YOUR COMFORT ZONE

What you do online should be fun – don't do anything that makes you feel uncomfortable, unhappy or anxious. You have the right to set your own limits and no one has the right to try to persuade or bully you into doing anything you don't want to do.

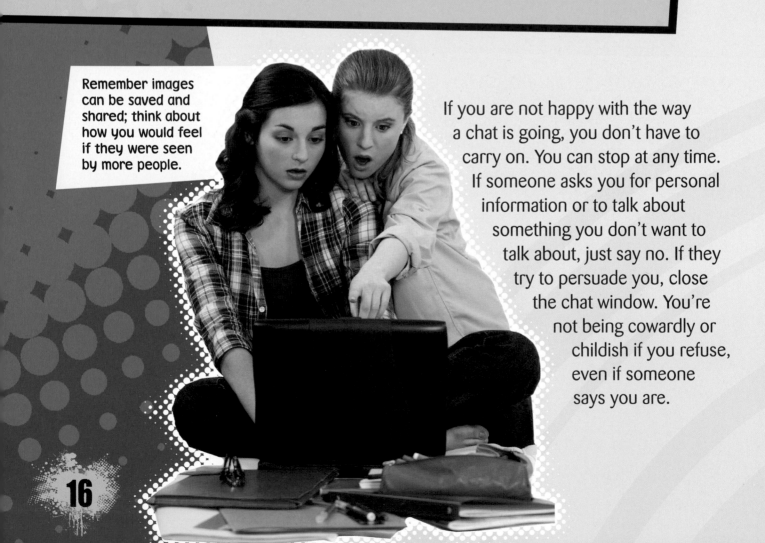

Remember images can be saved and shared; think about how you would feel if they were seen by more people.

If you are not happy with the way a chat is going, you don't have to carry on. You can stop at any time. If someone asks you for personal information or to talk about something you don't want to talk about, just say no. If they try to persuade you, close the chat window. You're not being cowardly or childish if you refuse, even if someone says you are.

16

Don't suffer alone. Show an adult if someone online asks you to do something that makes you feel uncomfortable.

When you use a webcam, think of it as if you are face to face with that person in the real world. Never do or say anything in front of a webcam that you wouldn't do or say if the other person were in front of you.

SAFETY TIP

You can stop chatting with someone who makes you uncomfortable, and you can block them so that they can't contact you again. As long as you haven't given them any other contact details, they won't be able to reach you in future.

TOO MUCH

Most young people enjoy online activities as part of life, but a few spend so much time online they forget about other important aspects of life. When going online replaces time with friends and family in the real world, it could be getting out of hand. Try to find a balance between having fun online, staying healthy and keeping up with your friends and schoolwork.

It's easy to get sucked into spending more and more time online, especially if you enjoy games or chatting to friends you don't see day-to-day. But if going online is your main out-of-school activity, it's time to take a careful look at how much time you are spending on it.

Don't cut yourself off from the real world – going online should be part of life, not all of it!

SAFETY TIP

Take regular breaks from looking at the screen to give your eyes and brain a rest. Try a day a week with no online time – if you find it too hard, it's time to cut down.

It's possible to become addicted to online activity. If you are staying up late at night, forgetting to wash or change your clothes, skipping proper meals and even missing school, it's certainly time to get help. You can ask a parent, a school counsellor or a doctor to help you sort things out.

Headaches, problems sleeping or other signs of illness can be a clue that you are using the computer too much.

CLICK WITH CARE

The internet is used by people with widely varying interests. Some adults enjoy looking at or reading about things that are not suitable for young people. There is a lot of material online that you might find upsetting. Some is illegal, but a lot is just unpleasant.

If you come across something you don't like online, it's easy to close the page and move on – but tell someone if you're upset.

Some adult material is sexual, and some of that is **pornography**. Young people sometimes look for pornography because they are curious about sex, but it does not give an accurate, responsible or realistic view of sex. To find out about your body and sexuality, it's better to use proper educational materials, or ask a trustworthy adult.

SAFETY TIP

If you use a search engine to look for information, read the little block of text about the pages found before clicking on the link. This helps you find suitable pages.

Anyone can post material online, and no one is checking whether it's true or decent. Some online information is wrong, either because it's posted to mislead people or because someone just hasn't checked the facts. Political groups often present opinions as facts. Find trustworthy sources if you are looking for information online.

You might be able to set your computer to block some types of images. Ask a grown-up to help you change settings.

GOING VIRAL

Anything that is uploaded to a website or sent by email or text message can be forwarded or copied. It can whizz round the world in seconds and you can never get it back. Don't upload or email anything that you wouldn't want to be made public, as you can never be sure it won't be shared or, worse still, **go viral**.

Think about how you would feel if everyone were to see the photos and messages you have uploaded.

You don't have to let people take photos or videos of you messing around. If you don't want someone to share photos or videos they have taken, say so. Sometimes people fall out with friends. It's best if your friends don't have anything embarrassing they could share if you had an argument.

SAFETY TIP

Check all the photos and videos you have posted online and take down any that you wouldn't like to be public.

It can be very distressing if someone shares information or photos you consider private. It might just be embarrassing, but it might get you into trouble at school or home. Information on the internet can stay there forever. Something that seems funny now might not be so funny later when you need a job or college place.

If you want to upload a photo of friends, check they are happy for you to tag them. If in doubt, don't. They can always tag themselves if they want to.

INFECTED COMPUTER

If you are careless online, you can put your computer at risk. You could lose your data or have your computer or online accounts hijacked by **malware** – software written to cause harm. Malware can change your settings, delete your data or use your computer to send out more malware or spam (unwanted email).

Sometimes hackers can hijack your webcam and take photos without your knowledge.

Some free software hides malware – software that will harm your computer. Ask an adult before **downloading** anything. Your computer can also be infected from an email **attachment**, so don't open attachments you aren't expecting. And if your computer is not protected, some dodgy websites can even drop bits of malware onto it without you knowing. Tell an adult if you get a pop-up message about your **anti-virus software**, or if you think something is wrong.

SAFETY TIP

Never download illegal copies of music, videos or books. Not only are you breaking the law, but some 'torrent' or file-sharing sites download malware with or instead of the files you want.

'Phishing' emails are messages that ask you to log into your account (such as your social networking account). They are sent by criminals to try to get you to log into a fake copy of the site. Then they record the login details you use on the site and use them to get into your real account. Only log into your accounts directly from the web page – never follow an email link to log in.

You might not realize if your computer becomes infected. Anti-malware software is important.

25

DEALING WITH PROBLEMS

Anyone can have problems online – it can happen even if you have been careful. Don't be afraid or embarrassed to ask for help – like most things, problems online are easier to sort out if you get help quickly, before things become worse.

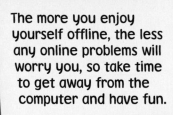

The more you enjoy yourself offline, the less any online problems will worry you, so take time to get away from the computer and have fun.

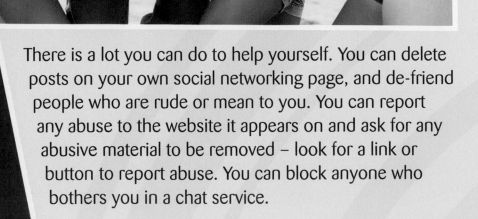

There is a lot you can do to help yourself. You can delete posts on your own social networking page, and de-friend people who are rude or mean to you. You can report any abuse to the website it appears on and ask for any abusive material to be removed – look for a link or button to report abuse. You can block anyone who bothers you in a chat service.

SAFETY TIP

It's not just about you: if you get help to stop a criminal or cyberbully, you help the people they would have hurt in the future, too. Be responsible, and report abuse.

If you have problems you can't sort out, or if something online has upset you, tell a responsible adult about it. You might tell a parent or a teacher, or perhaps a school counsellor. If the matter is serious enough to involve the police, they will be kind and supportive.

There are plenty of people who will be willing to take your problems seriously and help you - just ask!

SUMMARIZER

Here's a reminder of the most important points made in the book. Look back if you want to see more information about anything.

1 Cyberbullying is any repeated unkind behaviour online that is intended to upset someone.

2 Keep your passwords secret. If you think someone knows a password, change it.

3 It's best not to accept people you don't know as friends. In particular, don't chat online with people you don't know.

4 Be careful what you share online. Never give out personal details that would help someone to find you in the real world.

5 Think before uploading or sharing any photos or videos. Remember they could be passed on to people you wouldn't want to see them – it's impossible to get back something that has been passed on.

6 You can always stop a chat session if you are uncomfortable with anything that is happening.

7 You can block someone if you don't want them to contact you again.

8 Search carefully and check the text information about a web page before following the link – this will help you to avoid upsetting material.

9 If you want information about health and sexuality, ask an adult or look in an educational book for suitable and accurate information – don't search online.

10 Ask a grown-up to check that your computer is properly protected against malware.

11 If you are upset by something online, or have an online problem you can't solve alone, speak to a trusted adult.

12 Report any abuse to the website you find it on. You might be helping someone else as well as yourself.

GLOSSARY

abusive rude, nasty and aggressive

account an arrangement with an online company that allows you to send email, buy goods or join a group

anti-virus software software that protects your computer from malware from the internet

attachment a file sent with an email, usually shown as a paperclip

cyberbully a person who bullies someone online

de-friend delete a person you have accepted as a friend on a social media site

disrupt make it hard for something to carry on as normal

downloading copying an internet file onto your computer

hijack take over without permission

go viral when something on the internet becomes really popular to look at and share with others

infected affected by damaging malware

malware software created to damage or take information from a computer, such as a virus

personal information your name, address, date of birth and other details about you

pornography images with sexual content

privacy settings the way to control what you share with others online

ridiculing making fun of

target something that someone aims at

upload copy a photo or file from your computer onto a website on the internet

webcam a camera attached to or inside a computer

FURTHER INFORMATION

Websites

kids.usa.gov/online-safety/index.shtml
Links to lots of good resources about online safety.

tweenangels.org/
Online safety advice and materials specifically for 7 to 12-year-olds.

www.kidsmart.org.uk/
Lots of advice on how to stay safe online.

www.thinkuknow.co.uk
Information, games, videos and factsheets to help you think about safety online and enjoy using the internet safely.

Books

Bullied in Cyberspace, **Anne Rooney**, World Book, 2014

Cyberbullying, **Lucia Raatma**, Scholastic, 2013

Cyberbullying, **Heather Schwartz**, Capstone Press, 2013

Internet Safety, **Anne Rooney**, Franklin Watts, 2011

Safe Social Networking, **Heather Schwartz**, Capstone Press, 2013

Helplines

www.beatbullying.org/
Speak to a person your own age about any problems you have online (UK).

www.ceop.police.uk/safety-centre/
CEOP is part of the UK police service that exists to help keep young people safe online. You can report any abuse or anything that makes you feel uncomfortable through this website (UK).

www.childline.org.uk/ or 0800 1111
Get help with any online or offline abuse or bullying (UK).

www.kidshelp.com.au/kids/ or 1800 55 1800
Get help with any type of problem (Australia).

INDEX

SERIES CONTENTS

Keeping Safe around Alcohol, Drugs and Cigarettes
- Avoiding Harm from Drink, Drugs and Cigarettes
- Being Around Drink, Drugs and Cigarettes
- About Alcohol • Alcohol Around You • Alcohol and You
- Cigarettes and Addiction • Dangers of Smoking
- Avoiding Smoke • About Drugs • Dangers of Drug Misuse
- Dangers to You • Taking a Stand

Keeping Safe on the Street
- Be Street Smart • Know Your Journey
- Stay Aware • Dog Dangers • Stranger Danger
- Trouble on the Streets • Safe Cycling
- Safe Skateboarding • Keep Away from Building Sites
- Keep Away from Rail Tracks
- Stay Safe on Public Transport • After Dark

Keeping Safe Online
- Having a Happy Online Life • Cyberbullying
- Using Social Media Safely • Share Carefully
- Keep Your Information Safe • Online Chat
- Stay in Your Comfort Zone • Too Much
- Click With Care • Going Viral • Infected Computer
- Dealing With Problems

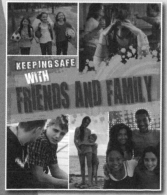

Keeping Safe with Friends and Family
- Making Decisions • Helping Out • Emergency!
- Anger and Arguments • Family Matters • Pet Safety
- Peer Pressure • Safety at Home • Out with Friends
- Going to Friends' Houses • Your Body Belongs to You
- Good Secrets and Bad Secrets